A SPECIAL DELIVERY...
...FROM MY HEART TO YOURS
BY HEIDI MARKISH

MW00681346

Welcome to my first book! Exactly 10 years ago I was preparing to graduate from Duquesne University with a degree in elementary education. If someone would have told me then that in 10 years I would be a stay at home Mom, running a successful pattern business, and loving every minute of it, I would have never believed them. But this is exactly what I am doing. After teaching grade school for 6 years I took the chance to follow a different path. Every step down this new path has been a rewarding one. I have met many wonderful people, from Karen and Mary Ellen at the Country Craft Cupboard in Berlin, OH, to all my fellow painters who inspire me with their words of encouragement and praise. A big thanks to all of you.

I would like to dedicate this book to my wonderful family. First of all to my two year old daughter, Lauren, for her patience and unconditional love. Being able to work out of my home in order to be with her is a true blessing. To my mom who I could never thank enough for all her help and guidance. She's my very "bestest" friend and I love her more than words can say. A big thank you to my Dad for always making me feel that I can achieve anything (he's getting pretty good at folding those patterns too). And to my husband Craig, though I don't say it enough, I appreciate your help more than you know. You make my life complete and I love you dearly.

I would like to thank Provo Craft for giving me this great opportunity. And to Barbara Sanderson...she is so kind and helpful even when I bug her with the silliest of questions...thank you so very much!

Published by Provo Craft
Provo, Utah
Managing Editor, Clella Gustin
Design and Book Coordinator,
Barbara Sanderson
Photography by Craig Young

From my heart to yours...
Heidi

For a Catalog of my individual pattern packets, please write to :
FROM MY HEART TO YOURS
27 ROBERTS DR.
BURGETTSTOWN, PA 15021
Phone: 724-947-5093

TABLE OF CONTENTS

For your convenience, Provo Craft computer numbers have been listed. Warehouse orders may be placed at the Provo Craft Warehouse, 1-800-937-7686, 285 East 900 South, Provo, Utah 84606. If you do not have a wholesale account, you may order retail from the Provo Craft Shipping Department at 1-800-563-8679, 295 West Center Street, Provo, Utah 84601.

Alternate wood sources for wood not being cut by Provo Craft are: A & P Craft Supply, 1-800-748-5090, 850 West 200 South, Lindon, Utah 84042, and Hansens' Wood Crafts, 1-801-227-7189, 460 East 1070 South, Orem, Utah 84097.

ISBN 158050-040-4

Provo Craft will make every effort to maintain an inventory of those wood items shown in our books; however, we cannot guarantee that they will be available for the sales life of the book.

GENERAL INSTRUCTIONS

WOOD PREPARATION

*SANDING - Sand all the wood pieces until they are smooth to the touch. (I use an electric, handheld, sander. with medium grit sandpaper.) Remove dust with a damp cloth. I choose not to seal my wood.

*DRILLING - Pre-drill any necessary holes as indicated on individual patterns.

*TRANSFERRING PATTERN TO WOOD - Transfer the pattern to tracing paper. When finished, place the tracing paper over the wood project, taping it in place. Carefully slide graphite paper under the tracing paper. Use a stylus or sharp pencil and lightly trace over the design.

BRUSHES AND PAINTING TECHNIQUES

*BASECOATING - I use 1" & 2" foam brushes. The size will depend on the area to be painted. I apply two coats of paint. For very small areas I use Loew-Cornell 7300 shader #4.

*STRIPES & PLAIDS - Loew-Cornell Series 7300 shader #6 and #8. Thin paint to ink consistency so it will flow evenly.

*LINEWORK - Loew-Cornell Series 7350 liner #10/0. Thin paint to ink consistency.

*SHADING - Loew-Cornell Series 7400 angular 3/8 (technique: dip bristles into clean water and blot off on a paper towel. Dip corner of angular brush into the paint and blend onto a palette. Hold brush flat against surface and drag along line that is to be shaded. When paint starts to fade, repeat the steps.)

*HIGHLIGHTING - Loew-Cornell #6 stencil brush and a Spouncer by Plaid. Use the stencil brush to high light small areas in the project. Use the spouncer to highlight around the edge of the project. I do this by "scraping" the spouncer along the edges. For highlighting lines, use Loew-Cornell 7400 angular 3/8. (Same technique as shading but using a lighter color than the basecoat.)

*STENCILING & DRYBRUSHING - Loew-Cornell #6 stencil brush. Use very little paint for this. Brush out excess paint onto a paper towel before you start.

*SPECKLING - Use an old toothbrush. Dip brush into some water and shake off excess. Dip the end of the bristles into some paint. Point brush head towards project and drag thumb across bristles. The more water you use, the larger the spatters.

*DOTS - I use a stylus for small dots and the end of a paint brush for larger dots.

PAINTS and STAINS

*PAINTS - All paints used in this book are Ceramcoat by Delta.

*STAINING - I use Minwax's Early American on all my projects. Technique: Use an old rag to apply stain to entire project. Before it dries, quickly wipe stain off with another old rag. Apply a second coat if you want the project to appear even darker.

*ANTIQUING - I use antiquing gel by Delta. My favorite color is the Dark Brown. Where the antiquing is done on Antique White areas in these projects, a few drops of Black have been added to the Dark Brown. Technique: Place a small amount of gel onto a paper plate. I use an old sock and with my pointing finger I rub the gel around the edges of my project. Wipe any excess gel off with a clean part of the sock.

FINISHING TECHNIQUES

*LETTERING - For thin lines I use a liner paint brush but for most of my lettering I use a 6mm line wood craft marker.

*APPLYING CHEEKS - On most of my projects, I use actual facial blush for the cheeks. I simply rub some blush onto my finger and I apply it to the project in a circular motion. (It will be the acrylic varnish that will seal in the cheeks.) If I don't use facial blush, I choose to dry-brush the cheeks.

*TEA-DYING - I use Rit-Dye (taupe) to achieve the antique look on fabric.

*SPRAY FINISH - I use Delta's acrylic satin finish spray (a very light coat).

THINK SNOW

(This wood is not available from Provo Craft.)

PALETTE:
CERAMCOAT BY DELTA
Antique White   Cinnamon   Black

SUPPLIES:
19 Gauge Wire, Small Piece of Homespun, Pencil with New Eraser, Facial Blush, Sawtooth Picture Hanger

WOODCUTTING HINTS:
The body is cut from 1" Pine. The arms and feet are cut from 1/2" Pine. The sign and nose are cut from 1/4" Poplar. Drill holes as marked on the pattern. Sand the wood and wipe it clean.

PAINTING INSTRUCTIONS:
ANTIQUE WHITE — Base the body, arms, feet, and sign.
CINNAMON — Base the patches. Thin the paint and add fringe to the patches. Paint the border around the sign.
BLACK — Base the nose. Use the pencil eraser and make dots to create buttons on the front. Shade around all edges. Dot the eyes and line the mouth. Paint the lines and dots on the paws. Paint the lettering on the sign. Add linework around the sign. Paint dots near the nose.
ANTIQUE WHITE — Paint lines and dots on the patches. Highlight the nose. Highlight the edge of the sign with the Spouncer as explained in the General Instructions.
BLACK —Paint the stitching lines on the patches.
PERMANENT BLACK LINING PEN —Line around the face, ears and body. Line the shadow lines on the lettering.

**NOTE: WHEN THE PAINT IS DRY, STAIN AND ANTIQUE THE ENTIRE PROJECT. THE INSIDE PART OF THE SIGN IS SHADED DURING THIS STEP AS EXPLAINED IN THE GENERAL INSTRUCTIONS.

ASSEMBLY:
Nail the sawtooth hanger to the back. Nail the feet to the body. Wire the sign to the arms and then wire the arms to the body. Glue a Homespun bow at the neckline. Apply Facial Blush to the cheeks, inner ears and along the paw markings. Dot highlights in the ears and line cross-hatching on the cheeks with Antique White. Attach the nose with wood glue. Lightly spray the project with acrylic spray

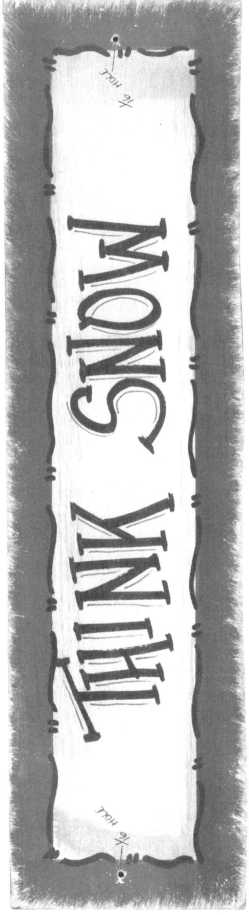

SUGAR & SPICE

(This wood is not available from Provo Craft.)

PALETTE:
CERAMCOAT BY DELTA
Spice Brown   Antique White   Black   Burgundy Rose   Trail Tan

SUPPLIES:
Homespun Material, Knit Material, Lace, 8" Doily
5 Small Buttons, 1 Medium Button, 3/8" Plug

WOODCUTTING HINTS:
The body and base are cut from 1" Pine. The arms and legs are cut from 3/8" plywood. Drill holes as indicated on the pattern. Sand the wood and wipe it clean with a damp cloth.

PAINTING INSTRUCTIONS:
SPICE BROWN — Base the body, arms, legs, and nose.
BURGUNDY ROSE — Dry brush the cheeks.
BLACK — Base the shoes. Dot the eyes and paint the mouth.
TRAIL TAN — Paint the laces on the shoes.
ANTIQUE WHITE — Paint the icing stripes on the face, arms, and legs. Highlight the nose. Speckle the entire project.

**NOTE: WHEN THE PAINT IS DRY, SAND THE EDGES TO EXPOSE THE WOOD. STAIN AND ANTIQUE THE ENTIRE PROJECT (THIS TECHNIQUE, AS EXPLAINED IN THE GENERAL INSTRUCTIONS, GIVES THE EFFECT OF SHADING.) LINE CROSS-HATCHING ON THE CHEEKS WITH ANTIQUE WHITE FOLLOWING THIS STEP.

Attach Body Here.

ASSEMBLY:
Attach the body to the base with 2" wood screws. (The body is placed on top of the base.) Wire arms to the body. Attach the nose with wood glue. Before attaching the legs, make the leggings by cutting two pieces of knit material 8" x 7". Fold each in half and stitch or hot glue the side seam. Slide leggings down each leg. Scrunch them down and secure with glue. Add a Homespun bow to each. Wire legs to the base. For the dress, cut a piece of Homespun 14" x 42" and a piece of lace 2-1/4" x 42". Glue or stitch the lace to the bottom of the dress. Run a large gathering stitch by hand at the top edge of the dress. Slide the dress on the body placing it just beneath where the arms are wired onto the body. Pull up the gathering stitch and tie off the ends. Secure the dress with glue. Cut the center out of the doily and slide it down over the head. Secure with glue. Add a bow at the neckline along with a fancy button. For the bow on the head, rip a piece of Homespun 2" wide and create a bow. For the bows on the legs, make them out of a strip 1-1/2" wide. Add some lace and a button to each bow. Space them out as you wish on the bottom of the dress and secure with hot glue. Lightly spray with acrylic varnish.

MITTEN GARLAND
11-2219

PALETTE:
CERAMCOAT BY DELTA
Candy Bar Brown   Nightfall Blue   Golden Brown
Woodland Night Green   Antique White   Spice Brown
Black   Terra Cotta   Trail Tan   Burgundy Rose

SUPPLIES:
Jute, 5 Wooden Spools (3/4" X 1"), Variety of Homespun Material, Wood Glue

WOODCUTTING HINTS:
The four mittens are cut from 1/2" Pine. The star, snowman, heart and gingerbread boy are cut from 1/4" Pine.
Drill holes as marked on the pattern. Sand the wood and wipe it clean with a damp cloth.

PAINTING INSTRUCTIONS:
ANTIQUE WHITE — Base the snowman.
CANDY BAR BROWN — Base one mitten and the heart. Base two patches on the snowman.
NIGHTFALL BLUE — Base one mitten and one patch on the snowman.
GOLDEN BROWN — Base one mitten and the star. Paint three stars on the snowman.
WOODLAND NIGHT GREEN — Base one mitten and one patch on the snowman.
SPICE BROWN — Base the gingerbread boy.
BURGUNDY ROSE — Dry brush cheeks on the snowman and gingerbread boy.
ANTIQUE WHITE — Paint lettering on the mittens. Make dots on the mittens. Paint icing on the ginger-
   bread boy. Dot buttons on the gingerbread boy. Highlight the heart. Float a highlight along the bottom edge
   of the cuff. Dot the red patches and line plaid on the green patch on the snowman. Using a Spouncer, brush
   highlights around the edge of the heart. Speckle the project.
BLACK — Dot eyes and paint mouths on the snowman and gingerbread boy.
TERRA COTTA —Paint the nose on the snowman.
TRAIL TAN —Highlight the mittens.
PERMANENT BLACK LINING PEN — Line the snowman's nose, eyebrows and around his body as shown in the
   picture.

**NOTE: WHEN PAINT IS DRY, STAIN AND ANTIQUE THE ENTIRE PROJECT. (DON'T FORGET TO STAIN THE
WOODEN SPOOLS.) THIS TECHNIQUE, AS EXPLAINED IN THE GENERAL INSTRUCTIONS, GIVES THE EFFECT
OF SHADING.

ASSEMBLY:
Use jute to connect the mittens. Cut three sections of jute 10" long and two sections about 15" long. The 15"
pieces will be used on the ends and the other three will be in the middle. Tie a loop at the end of each 15" sec-
tion. Slide a wooden spool on the unlooped end. Attach the unlooped end to the first and last mitten. Next, take
the three 10" sections and slide a spool onto each one. Finish attaching the other mittens. Rip 15 strips of
Homespun 1-1/4" x 6". Do this with four different colors of Homespun. Tie these strips around the jute. (keep the
spools centered between the mittens). Tie a Homespun scarf around the snowman's neck. Use wood glue to
attach the star, snowman, heart and gingerbread boy. Lightly spray the mittens with acrylic spray.

"CHRISTMAS TREES" SNOWMAN
11-2225

PALETTE:
CERAMCOAT BY DELTA
Antique White   Black   Woodland Night Green
Terra Cotta   Golden Brown   Mendocino Red

SUPPLIES:
Piece of an Old Sweater, 1 Wooden Star, 3 Pre-cut Birds,
Greenery & Berries, 3/16" Checkerboard Stencil, Hot Glue,
Wood Glue, Finishing Nails, Facial Blush, (2) 2" Wood Screws

© 1998 Heidi Markish

Pattern pieces for Mitten Garland

1/8 HOLE   1/8 HOLE

KEEP YOUR HEART WARM

8

"CHRISTMAS TREES" SNOWMAN

WOODCUTTING HINTS:
Body is cut from 1" Pine. The trees, nose and sign are cut from 1/4" wood. The birds and star are cut from 3/8" wood. Base is cut from 1" Pine (round the edges). I chose to rout the base. Sand the wood and wipe it clean with a damp cloth.

PAINTING INSTRUCTIONS:
WOODLAND NIGHT GREEN — Base the trees.
TERRA COTTA — Base the nose.
GOLDEN BROWN — Base the sign and star.
MENDOCINO RED — Base the birds.
BLACK — Base the hat.
ANTIQUE WHITE — Basecoat the body and base. Highlight the hat, trees and birds. Stencil the checkerboard design onto the sign. Paint the lettering on the small tree.
BLACK — Dot the eyes. Paint the lettering on the sign. Paint the birds' beaks and dot their eyes.
ANTIQUE WHITE — Dot tiny highlights in the eyes. Speckle the entire project. Using the Spouncer, highlight here and there on the trees, hat and sign.
PERMANENT BLACK LINING PEN — Line the eyebrows, the stitches on the mouth, and around the nose, body and sign.

**NOTE: WHEN THE PAINT IS DRY, STAIN AND ANTIQUE THE ENTIRE PROJECT. (THIS TECHNIQUE, AS EXPLAINED IN THE GENERAL INSTRUCTIONS, GIVES THE EFFECT OF SHADING.)

ASSEMBLY:
From an old sweater, cut out a 16" x 9" piece. Fold in half and stitch or hot glue the long side. Turn right side out and fold down the top two times. Slide the sweater over the snowman's head and secure with hot glue. Add greenery and berries near the neckline. Nail the two large trees to the back of the body with finishing nails. Using wood glue, attach the star, sign, and birds. Hot glue the small tree to the front of the sweater. Attach the nose with wood glue. Use the 2" wood screws and attach the base to the body. Lightly spray the project with acrylic spray.

Example of Base
Base for "Trees for Sale." 15" x 5". Round the 2 sides. Router the edge.

HIT THE SLOPES
11-2221

PALETTE:
CERAMCOAT BY DELTA
Antique White   Nightfall Blue   Cinnamon   Spice Brown   Trail Tan   Black
Terra Cotta   Midnight Blue

SUPPLIES:
Posterboard, Knit Material, Homespun Material, 2 Wooden Buttons (1"), Crochet Thread, 19 Gauge Wire, Finishing Nails, Small Amount of Stuffing, 1 Plastic Button, Hot Glue, (2) 2" Wood Screws, 1/4" Checkerboard Stencil, Facial Blush

WOODCUTTING HINTS:

The body is cut from 1" Pine. The mittens are cut from 3/8" Pine. The nose and sign are cut from 1/4" wood. Drill any holes that are marked on the pattern. Sand the wood and wipe it clean with a damp cloth. The edges of the base are rounded with a router.

PAINTING INSTRUCTIONS:

ANTIQUE WHITE —Basecoat the body and base.

NIGHTFALL BLUE — Base the vest.

TRAIL TAN —Base the sign.

TERRA COTTA — Base the nose.

CINNAMON — Base the mittens. Thin the paint and apply the wide lines on the vest. Stencil the checker board design on the sign.

SPICE BROWN — Base the skis.

BLACK — Base the wooden buttons. Paint the lettering on the sign. Paint the eyes.

MIDNIGHT BLUE — Line narrow lines on each side of the wide plaid lines on the vest.

ANTIQUE WHITE — Paint snowflakes on the skis and mittens. Paint double thin plaid lines on the vest. Float a highlight on the cuff of the mittens. Dot a highlight in the eyes. Use a Spouncer to dry brush around the edges of the skis. Speckle the entire project.

PERMANENT BLACK LINING PEN — Line around the sign, around the snowman's body, and along the edge of the vest. Line the eyebrows.

** NOTE: WHEN PAINT IS DRY, STAIN AND ANTIQUE THE ENTIRE PROJECT USING A FEW DROPS OF BLACK PAINT IN THE DARK BROWN AS NOTED IN THE GENERAL INSTRUCTIONS.

ASSEMBLY:

Cut the two skis from posterboard and paint them according to the instructions above. For the hat, cut a piece of knit material 8" x 5-1/2". Fold in half and hot glue or stitch down the side. Turn right side out and fold up the bottom edge two times. Hot glue the hat on the head. Add a little stuffing down in the hat. Tie off the top with crochet thread. Cut slits in the top, then add a Homespun bow. For the scarf, cut a piece of knit material 2" x 36" and a piece of Homespun 1-1/4" x 36". Place the piece of Homespun on top of the knit material. Stitch or hot glue down the edges of the Homespun. Cut a piece of 19 gauge wire 36" long and feed it through the two layers on the scarf. Wrap the scarf around his neck and secure with hot glue. Bend the ends of the scarf to make it appear that it is flowing in the wind. Wire the sign to the snowman's left mitten. Position the two skis and secure with small finishing nails. Nail on the two mittens. Thread the two wooden buttons with crochet thread. Nail them to the vest. Apply cheeks with Facial Blush. Line cross-hatching on the cheeks with Antique White. Line, dot and stitch the mouth with Black. Attach the nose with wood glue. Glue the button to the scarf. Use the 2" wood screws and attach the base to the body. Lightly spray the project with acrylic spray.

Example of Base.

Base for " Hit The Slopes"
10" X 5" Round the 2 Sides.
Router the Edge.

"LETTERS FOR SANTA" SNOWMAN
11-2220

PALETTE:
CERAMCOAT BY DELTA
Antique White   Black Green   Trail Tan   Terra Cotta
Black   Barn Red   Golden Brown

SUPPLIES:
Burlap Material,   Knit Material,   Homespun Material,
Spanish Moss, Greenery, Dried Flowers & Berries, Jute,
White Posterboard, Manila Envelope, 1 Button, 3 Wooden
Stars, 1/2" & 3/16" Checkerboard Stencil, Small Amount
of Stuffing, Finishing Nails, Hot Glue, Wood Glue,
Facial Blush, Sawtooth Hanger.

WOODCUTTING HINTS:
The body is cut from 1" Pine. The arms are cut from 1/2" Pine. The sign and
nose are cut from 1/4" wood. Sand the wood and wipe it clean with a damp
cloth.

PAINTING INSTRUCTIONS:
BARN RED — Base the sign.
TERRA COTTA — Base the nose.
BLACK GREEN — Base the mittens. Stencil the
     checkerboard on the sign.
ANTIQUE WHITE — Base the body and arms. Paint the
     dots and highlights on the mittens and line the cuffs.
GOLDEN BROWN — Base the stars.
TRAIL TAN — Stencil the checkerboard on the body and
     arms. Paint the lettering on the sign.
BLACK — Dot the eyes.
ANTIQUE WHITE — Speckle the entire project.
PERMANENT BLACK LINING PEN — Line the eyebrows.
     Line around the body and arms.

** **NOTE:** WHEN THE PAINT IS DRY, SAND THE
EDGES TO EXPOSE THE WOOD. STAIN AND
ANTIQUE THE ENTIRE PROJECT. THIS TECHNIQUE,
AS EXPLAINED IN THE GENERAL INSTRUCTIONS,
GIVES THE EFFECT OF SHADING.

ASSEMBLY:
Cut a piece of burlap 12" x 8". Fold in half and hot glue the side and bottom. Turn the bag right side out and fold
down the top 1-1/4" then 1-1/4" again. Stuff the bottom of the bag with stuffing, glue Spanish Moss on top of
stuffing, glue a jute bow to the front of the bag, and glue the button to the bow. Next make the letters to Santa
by cutting 1-3/4" x 3-1/4" rectangles from white posterboard and the manila envelope. Draw a heart for the
"stamp" and address the envelopes. Glue letters, greenery, dried flowers and berries into the bag. For the hat,
cut a piece of knit material 10" x 8". Fold in half and glue or stitch the side seam. Turn right side out and roll up
the bottom of the hat two times. Place on his head and tack with glue. Add a small amount of stuffing down in
the hat and tie off the top with jute. Glue a Homespun bow on top of the jute and cut slits in the top of the
hat. For the scarf, cut a piece of Homespun 1-1/2" x 20" and a piece of knit material 2" x 20". Glue or stitch the
Homespun on top of the knit material. Trim the sides of the scarf and wrap around his neck. Tack with glue. Nail
a sawtooth hanger to the back. Nail the arms to the body and hot glue the bag between the mittens. Nail on
the three wooden stars. Apply Facial Blush to the cheeks and attach the nose with wood glue. Line, dot and
stitch the mouth with Black. Line cross-hatching on the cheeks with Antique White. Glue the sign to the bag.
Lightly spray the entire snowman with acrylic satin finish spray.

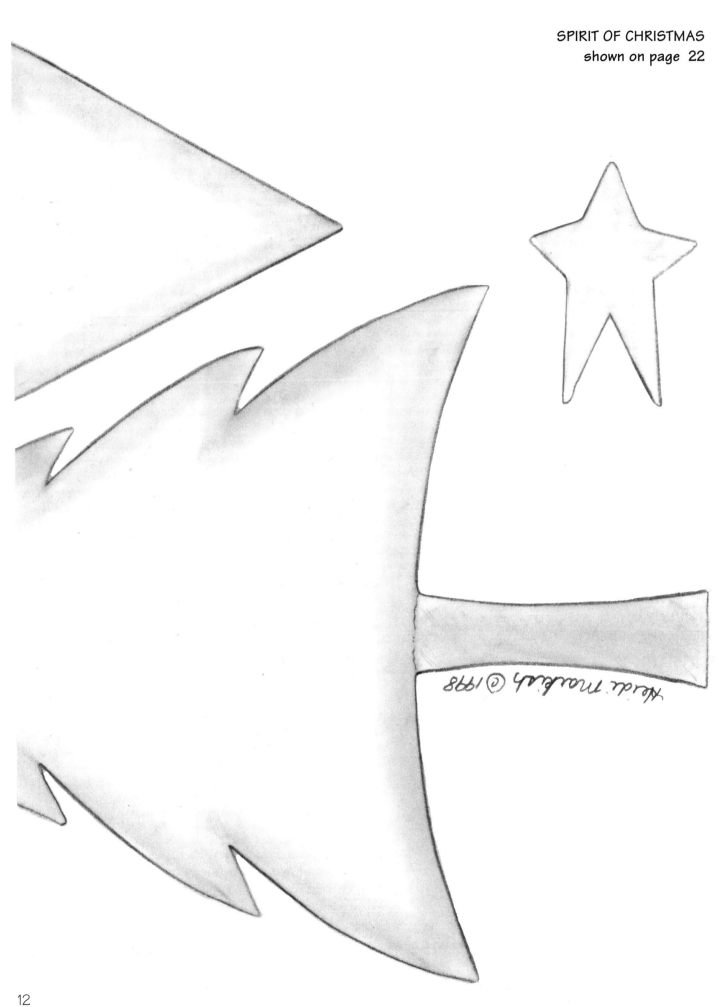

Heidi Markish © 1998

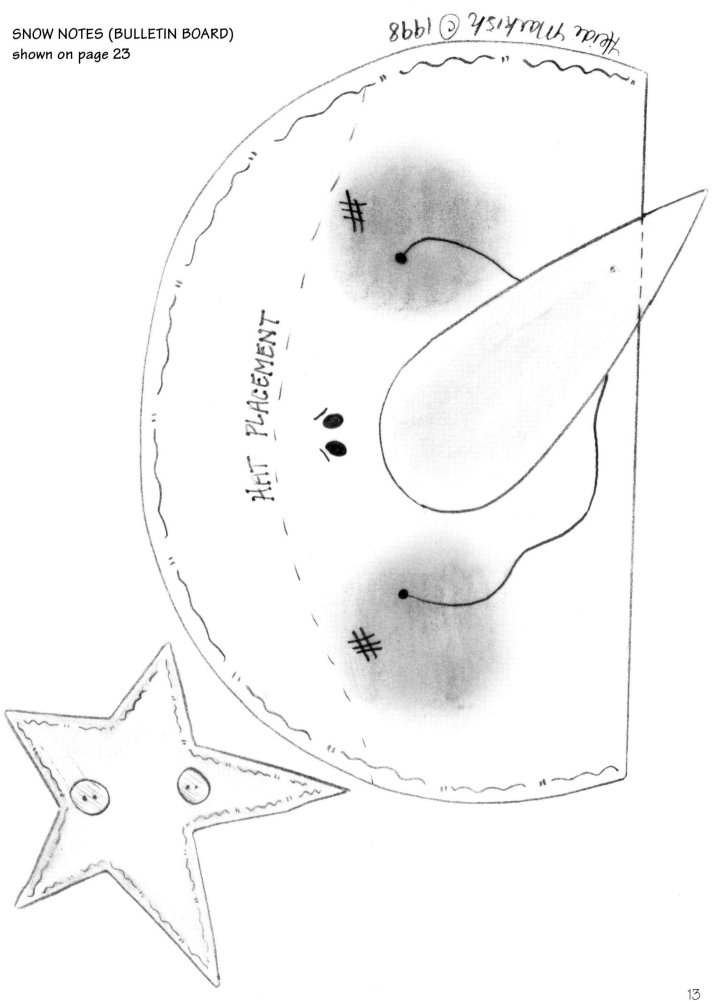

$5 COOKIES... $5

5¢ COOKIES
shown on page 19

$5
COOKIES...
$5

¹/₁₆ DRILL HOLE

¹/₁₆ DRILL HOLE

HIT THE
SLOPES

¹/₁₆

¹/₁₆

Hit The Slopes
shown on page 10

CHRISTMAS
TREES

Christmas Trees For Sale
shown on page 9

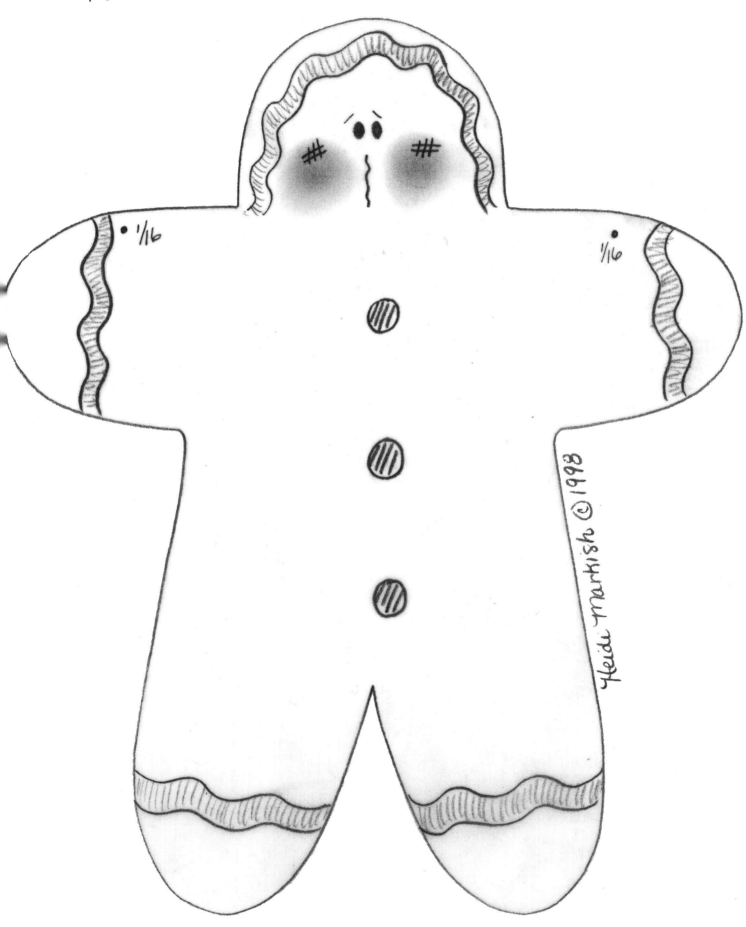

"PEACE ON EARTH" SANTA
11-2222

PALETTE:
CERAMCOAT BY DELTA
Maroon   Golden Brown   Black   Antique White   Trail Tan
Pine Green   Mendocino Red   Medium Flesh   Spice Brown

SUPPLIES:
Wavy Wool Hair by One & Only Creations, 3/8" Wooden Plug, 3/8" Checkerboard Stencil, Hot Glue, Wood Glue, Finishing Nails, 2" Wood Screws, Hair Pick and Hair Spray, Small and Medium Holly Stencils (I created my own by cutting them from a manila folder), Micron Pigma Pen (01), Facial Blush

WOODCUTTING INSTRUCTIONS :
The body and base are cut from 1" Pine. The base measures 12" x 5-1/2". I chose to rout the edge of the base. The arms and boots are cut from 1/2" Pine. The sign, hearts and star are cut from 1/8" Plywood. Sand the wood and wipe it clean with a damp cloth.

PAINTING INSTRUCTIONS:
**Before you begin to paint, trace the holly pattern onto a manila folder. Use an X-acto knife to cut it out. This will be your stencil.

MAROON— Base the coat and hat.
GOLDEN BROWN—Base the sign and star.
BLACK—Base the boots. Paint the lettering on the sign.
ANTIQUE WHITE— Base the coat trim. Paint the snowflakes.
TRAIL TAN— Stencil the checkerboard on the coat trim.
PINE GREEN— Stencil the holly.
MENDOCINO RED— Base the two small hearts. Dot the berries on the holly (I used a pencil eraser for this).
MEDIUM FLESH—Base the face and the nose (wooden plug).
SPICE BROWN — Base the mittens.
ANTIQUE WHITE — Stroke and dot highlights on the boots. Dot the snowflakes and the holly leave. Paint the eyebrows. Using the Spouncer, very lightly dry brush highlights on the edges of the hat, star, arms, mittens, sign, coat and shoes. Lightly stipple highlights on the holly leaves. Speckle the entire project.
PERMANENT BLACK LINING PEN — Line around the coat and sleeve trims. Line shadow lining on the left side and top of the letters. Draw the linework around the edge of the sign.

Example of Base.

Base for " Peace On Earth"
12" X 5½ "

**NOTE: WHEN PAINT IS DRY, SAND THE EDGES TO EXPOSE THE WOOD. STAIN AND ANTIQUE THE ENTIRE PROJECT. THE BASE IS ALSO STAINED WITH MINWAX EARLY AMERICAN.

ASSEMBLY:

Position the sign and star and nail them to the body using small finishing nails. Attach the hearts to the sign with wood glue. Position the boots and arms. Nail or screw these onto the body. Apply Facial Blush to the cheeks and a little on the top of the nose. Highlight the cheeks and nose with Antique White. Attach the nose with wood glue. For the beard, take a handful of the wavy wool and "fluff" it up by using the hair pick. Keep working at it until the hair appears soft and puffy. Glue it in sections around the face. Add as much as you wish. When the hair is finished, spray it with hair spray and form it as you desire. Take a small piece from the remaining wavy wool and make a small knot in the center. This will be the mustache. Hot glue it just below the nose. Attach the base to the body using the 2" wood screws. Lightly spray the project with Acrylic varnish.

5 CENT COOKIES
11-2223

PALETTE:
CERAMCOAT BY DELTA:
Spice Brown   Antique White   Cinnamon   Black   Burgundy Rose

SUPPLIES:
19 Gauge Wire, 1/2" Wooden Plugs (3), Cotton Lace, Homespun Material, Hot Glue, Wood Glue

WOODCUTTING HINTS:
The gingerbread and sign are cut from 1/4" Plywood. Drill holes as marked on the pattern. Sand the wood and wipe it clean with a damp cloth.

PAINTING INSTRUCTIONS:
SPICE BROWN — Base the gingerbread man.
ANTIQUE WHITE — Base the sign. Paint icing on the gingerbread man.
CINNAMON — Paint the outer edge of the sign. Speckle the sign.
BURGUNDY ROSE — Dry brush the cheeks.
BLACK — Base the wooden plugs. Add linework to the sign. Paint the lettering on the sign. Dot the eyes and paint the mouth and eyebrows.
ANTIQUE WHITE — Using the Spouncer technique in the General Instructions, highlight the buttons and around the edge of the sign. Dot tiny highlights in the eyes. Stroke highlights on the buttons. Very lightly stipple highlights on the cheeks. Speckle everything.

**NOTE: WHEN the PAINT IS DRY, SAND THE EDGES OF THE PROJECT TO EXPOSE THE WOOD. STAIN AND ANTIQUE THE ENTIRE PROJECT. (THIS TECHNIQUE, AS EXPLAINED IN THE GENERAL INSTRUCTIONS, GIVES THE EFFECT OF SHADING.) LINE THE CROSS-HATCHING ON THE CHEEKS WITH ANTIQUE WHITE FOLLOWING THIS STEP.

ASSEMBLY:
Attach the buttons with wood glue. Wrap a piece of cotton lace around the neck and secure with hot glue. Add a Homespun bow at the neckline. Wire the gingerbread man to the sign. Add a wire hanger to the sign. Curl parts of the wire by wrapping it around a pencil. Tie a few strips of Homespun where the wire meets the sign. Lightly spray the project with acrylic spray.

STAR SANTA
11-2224

PALETTE:
CERAMCOAT BY DELTA
Mendocino Red   Medium Flesh   Black   Golden Brown
Trail Tan   Antique White

SUPPLIES:
Homespun (Black design), Wavy Wool by One & Only Creations, Greenery & Berries, One Button, Facial Blush, Hot Glue, Wood Glue, Hair Pick, Hair Spray, 19 Gauge Wire

WOODCUTTING HINTS:
The body and star are cut from 1/4" Plywood. Drill holes as marked on the pattern. Sand the wood and wipe it clean with a damp cloth.

PAINTING INSTRUCTIONS:
MENDOCINO RED — Base the body.
MEDIUM FLESH — Base the face.
BLACK — Paint the four tips of the star. Dot the eyes.
GOLDEN BROWN — Base the small star.
TRAIL TAN — Paint the laces on the boots. With a Spouncer dry brush high lights around the edges of the large star and the small star.
ANTIQUE WHITE —Paint the eyebrows. Dot highlights in the eyes. Speckle the entire project.

**NOTE: WHEN THE PAINT IS DRY, STAIN AND ANTIQUE THE ENTIRE PROJECT. THIS TECHNIQUE, AS EXPLAINED IN THE GENERAL INSTRUCTIONS, GIVES THE EFFECT OF SHADING.

ASSEMBLY:
Attach a wire hanger through holes in Santa's hands, curling the ends to secure in place. Attach the small star to the tip of the hat with wood glue. Rip a piece of Homespun 1-1/2" x 25" and tie it around Santa's waist. Tie it off with a bow. Slide greenery beneath the bow. Glue on berries. Secure the entire belt with hot glue. Add a button to the bow. Apply the cheeks with Facial Blush. Dot highlights in the cheeks with Antique White. For the hair, take a handful of the wavy wool and "fluff" it up with the hair pick. Keep working at it until the beard appears soft and puffy. Glue it in sections around the face. Add as much as you wish. When hair is finished, spray it with hair spray and form it as you desire. Take a small piece of the remaining wavy wool and make a small knot in the center. This will be the mustache. Glue the mustache just below the eyes. Lightly spray the entire project with acrylic spray.

1/16 HOLE

HOLIDAY HELP WANTED

1/16 HO

HOLIDAY HELP

(This wood is not available from Provo Craft.)

PALETTE:
CERAMCOAT BY DELTA:

Medium Flesh   Pine Green   Antique White   Tomato Spice   Black
Golden Brown   Burnt Sienna   Trail Tan

SUPPLIES:
Homespun Material, 4 Medium Jingle Bells, 5 Small Jingle Bells,
1 Wooden Star, 6" Medallion Doily, 19 Gauge Wire, Curly Hair by
One & Only Creations (Autumn Brown), Button, 3/8" Wooden Plug,
Rit Dye (Scarlet), Facial Blush, Hot Glue,   Wood Glue, Needle &
Thread, Hair Spray, 2" Wood Screws

WOODCUTTING HINTS:
The body and base are cut from 1" Pine. (I chose to rout the edge of
the base.) The arms are cut from 1/2" Pine. The sign and the star
are cut from 1/4" Pine. Drill any holes as marked on the pattern.
Sand the wood and wipe it clean with a damp cloth.

PAINTING INSTRUCTIONS:
MEDIUM FLESH — Base the face, hands and nose (wooden plug).
PINE GREEN — Base the hat and shoes.
ANTIQUE WHITE — Base the sleeves and body. Paint the laces on the
    shoes.
BLACK — Base the center of the sign. Dot the eyes and paint the mouth
    and eyebrows.
TOMATO SPICE — Paint the stripes on the arms and legs. Base the edge of
    the sign.
GOLDEN BROWN — Base the star.
BURNT SIENNA — Shade the face, ears and hands.
TRAIL TAN —Highlight the shoes.
ANTIQUE WHITE — Float a highlight around the center part of the sign.
    Highlight the nose. Add linework and line and dot the lettering on the
    sign. With a Spouncer, lightly dry brush the toes of the shoes.

**NOTE: WHEN PAINT IS DRY, STAIN AND ANTIQUE THE ENTIRE PROJECT.
THE BASE IS ALSO STAINED WITH MINWAX. THIS TECHNIQUE, AS
EXPLAINED IN THE GENERAL INSTRUCTIONS, GIVES THE EFFECT OF
SHADING.

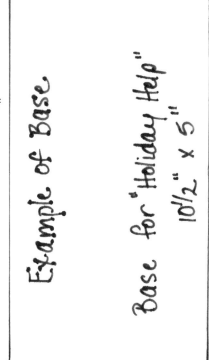

Example of Base

Base for "Holiday Help"
10½" x 5"

ASSEMBLY:
Line the center of the legs with Black. Apply the cheeks with Facial Blush. Line
cross-hatching on the cheeks and speckle the entire project with Antique White. Attach the nose and star with
wood glue. Wire the arms to the body. For the hair, take a small amount of the curly hair and rub it between your
hands. This will help it appear fuller. Attach it to the top of the head with hot glue. Lightly apply hair spray to
keep it in place. For the collar, dye the doily with the Rit Dye. (Add a very small amount of the dye in an old bucket. Boil some water and add it to the dye. Dip the doily until you achieve the color you like most. Let the doily
dry.) Cut the center out of the doily and set aside. For the outfit, cut a piece of Homespun 8-1/2" x 20". Cut a
zig zag design at the bottom edge. Make a large gathering stitch by hand at the top edge. Place the outfit onto
the body just below where the arms are wired to the body.

HOLIDAY HELP

Pull up the gathering thread and secure with hot glue. Slide the doily over the head and secure it with glue. Add a button at the neckline. Attach the small bells to the collar and the medium bells to the outfit. Rip a piece of matching Homespun 1" wide and make two bows to glue to the shoes. Wire the sign to the hands. Attach the body to the base using 2" wood screws. Lightly spray the project with acrylic varnish.

SPIRIT OF CHRISTMAS

(This wood is not available from Provo Craft.)

PALETTE:
CERAMCOAT BY DELTA
Barn Red   Pine Green   Golden Brown   Spice Brown   Trail Tan
Candy Bar Brown   Black

SUPPLIES:
4 Pre-cut Wooden Stars, 3 Different Colors of Homespun Material, Finishing Nails, Wood Glue, 1/2" Checkerboard Stencil

WOODCUTTING HINTS:
The plaque is cut from 3/8" Plywood, it measures 11" x 17". The outside top edge is rounded. The tree and star are cut from 1/4" Plywood. Drill a hole at each corner at the top of the plaque. Sand the wood and wipe it clean.

PAINTING INSTRUCTIONS:
*Measure a 1-1/4" border around the outer edge of the plaque.

BARN RED — Base the center of the plaque.
PINE GREEN — Base the outer edge of the plaque and the tree.
GOLDEN BROWN — Base all of the stars.
SPICE BROWN — Base the trunk of the tree.
TRAIL TAN — Stencil the checkerboard design around the outer border. With a Spouncer highlight the tree and stars. Paint the lettering.
CANDY BAR BROWN--Shade the center of the plaque.
BLACK — Add linework around the outer edge of the center. Line shadow lines on the lettering.
TRAIL TAN — Speckle the entire project.

**NOTE: WHEN PAINT IS DRY, STAIN AND ANTIQUE THE ENTIRE PROJECT. THIS TECHNIQUE, AS EXPLAINED IN THE GENERAL INSTRUCTIONS, GIVES THE EFFECT OF SHADING.

ASSEMBLY:
Rip the three colors of Homespun 1-1/2" x 40". Pinch the three ends together and feed through one of the drilled holes. Tie off the end into a knot to prevent it from sliding back out of the hole. Begin to braid the three strands until you reach a length you like. Pinch the ends and feed through the other drilled hole and tie off into a knot. Trim the ends as desired. For the small bows, rip the three colors of Homespun 1/2" wide. Nail or glue small bows to the tree. Attach the tree and outer stars to the plaque with finishing nails. Attach the star to the top of the tree with wood glue. Lightly spray the plaque with acrylic varnish.

SNOW NOTES (BULLETIN BOARD)

(This wood is not available from Provo Craft.)

PALETTE:
CERAMCOAT BY DELTA
Antique White   Terra Cotta   Barn Red   Midnight Blue
Golden Brown   Trail Tan   Black

SUPPLIES:
11" X 17" Bulletin Board, Old Sweater, Small Piece of Homespun, 1 Pre-cut Wooden Star, Small Amount of Stuffing, 4 Buttons, Finishing Nails, Regular Nails, Hot Glue, Facial Blush, Sawtooth Picture Hanger

WOODCUTTING HINTS:
The head is cut from 1" Pine. The mittens are cut from 1/2" Pine, The nose and stars are cut from 1/4" wood. The back support, which holds the head to the bulletin board, is cut from 1/8" wood and measures 7" x 1-3/8". Sand the wood and wipe it clean with a damp cloth.

PAINTING INSTRUCTIONS:
ANTIQUE WHITE — Base the head.
TERRA COTTA — Base the nose.
BARN RED — Base the frame on the bulletin board.
MIDNIGHT BLUE —Base the mittens.
GOLDEN BROWN — Base the stars.
TRAIL TAN — Paint the small snowflakes on the mittens. Highlight the mittens.
BLACK — Dot the eyes. Line the eyebrows.
PERMANENT BLACK LINING PEN — Line around the snowman's head.

**NOTE: WHEN PAINT IS DRY, STAIN AND ANTIQUE THE ENTIRE PROJECT. THIS TECHNIQUE, AS EXPLAINED IN THE GENERAL INSTRUCTIONS, GIVES THE EFFECT OF SHADING.

The patterns for the snowman and the stars are on page 13.

ASSEMBLY:
Attach the head to the bulletin board by placing the support behind the bottom part of the head and along the top edge of the bulletin board. Nail the support to the head and the top edge of the bulletin board. Nail mittens to the front of the bulletin board. For the hat, cut an 8" x 16" piece out of an old sweater. Fold in half and stitch or hot glue the side. Turn right side out and fold up the bottom edge two times. Glue to the top of the head. Add a little stuffing down inside the hat and tie off the top with some string. Glue a small Homespun bow near the top of the hat. For the scarf, cut a 2-1/2" x 20" piece out of the same sweater. Tie around the snowman's neck and secure with hot glue. Trim as desired. Apply the cheeks with Facial Blush. Line cross-hatching on the cheeks with Antique white. Line and dot the mouth with Black. Attach the nose with wood glue. Attach two large stars with finishing nails and glue two buttons to each star. Attach a small star to the brim of the hat with hot glue. Attach a sawtooth picture hanger to the back of the support. Speckle the entire project with Antique White. Lightly spray the entire project with acrylic spray.

"I BELIEVE" ANGEL
11-2226

PALETTE:
CERAMCOAT BY DELTA
Antique White   Medium Flesh   Black   Trail Tan   Pine Green
Burnt Sienna   Mendocino Red   Mocha

SUPPLIES:
Osnaburg Material, 6" Doily, 4" Grapevine Wreath, 3/4" Checkerboard
Stencil, Holly Stencil (I cut my own out of a manila folder), Homespun
Material, Facial Blush, Glitter Spray (Silver), Finishing Nails, Hot Glue,
19 Gauge Wire, Sawtooth Picture Hanger, Rit Dye (Taupe), One Small
Button

WOODCUTTING HINTS:
The angel's body is cut from 1" Pine. The arms are cut from 1/4" wood.
The star and wings are cut from 1/8" Plywood. Drill holes as marked on
the pattern. Sand the wood and wipe it clean with a damp cloth.

PAINTING INSTRUCTIONS:
 **Before you begin to paint, trace the holly pattern onto a manila fold-
er. Use an X-acto knife to cut it out. This becomes your stencil. (There
are two different sizes of the holly.)
ANTIQUE WHITE — Base the dress.
MEDIUM FLESH — Base the face, hands and legs.
BLACK — Base the shoes. Dot the eyes and paint the mouth. Line the
    eyebrows.
TRAIL TAN — Stencil the checkerboard design on the dress. Highlight the shoes.
PINE GREEN — Stencil the holly on the dress. Thin the paint and add the vines around the holly.
BURNT SIENNA —Shade the hands and legs.
MENDOCINO RED — Dot the berries on the holly. (I did this with a pencil eraser.)
BLACK — Paint the lettering on the star.
ANTIQUE WHITE — Paint the laces in the shoes. Highlight the holly leaves. Dot highlights on the hands
    and berries. Speckle the star and the wings.
PERMANENT BLACK LINING PEN — Line around the star and wings as shown on the pattern.

NOTE: WHEN PAINT IS DRY, STAIN AND ANTIQUE THE ENTIRE PROJECT. THIS TECHNIQUE, AS
EXPLAINED IN THE GENERAL INSTRUCTIONS, GIVES THE EFFECT OF SHADING.

ASSEMBLY:
Lightly spray the wings and star with the Silver glitter spray. Wire the star to the arms and then the arms to
the body. Cut the center out of the doily and slide it over her head. Secure it with glue. Add a bow and button
to the neckline. Nail wings to the back. Add a sawtooth hanger on the back. For the hair, cut six layers of
Osnaburg 9" x 2-1/2" wide. Stack the six layers and stitch down the center two times. Next, cut 1/2" wide slits
up to the stitching line. (Make sure you don't cut into the stitching line.) Cut these slits on both sides. Next,
take a small amount of the Rit Dye and add it to an old pot or bucket. Add a little boiling water and stir. Dip
the Osnaburg hair into the dye until you achieve a color you like. The longer the hair remains in the dye, the darker it will become. Spin the hair in a washer to remove excess water. Throw the hair in the dryer to dry (this will
give it a ruffled look). Be sure to clean out your washer and dryer when this is done because this hair can be
messy! Hot glue the hair to the head. Apply Facial Blush to the cheeks. Line cross-hatching on the cheeks with
Antique White. Nail and hot glue the wreath to the head. Lightly spray the project with acrylic spray.

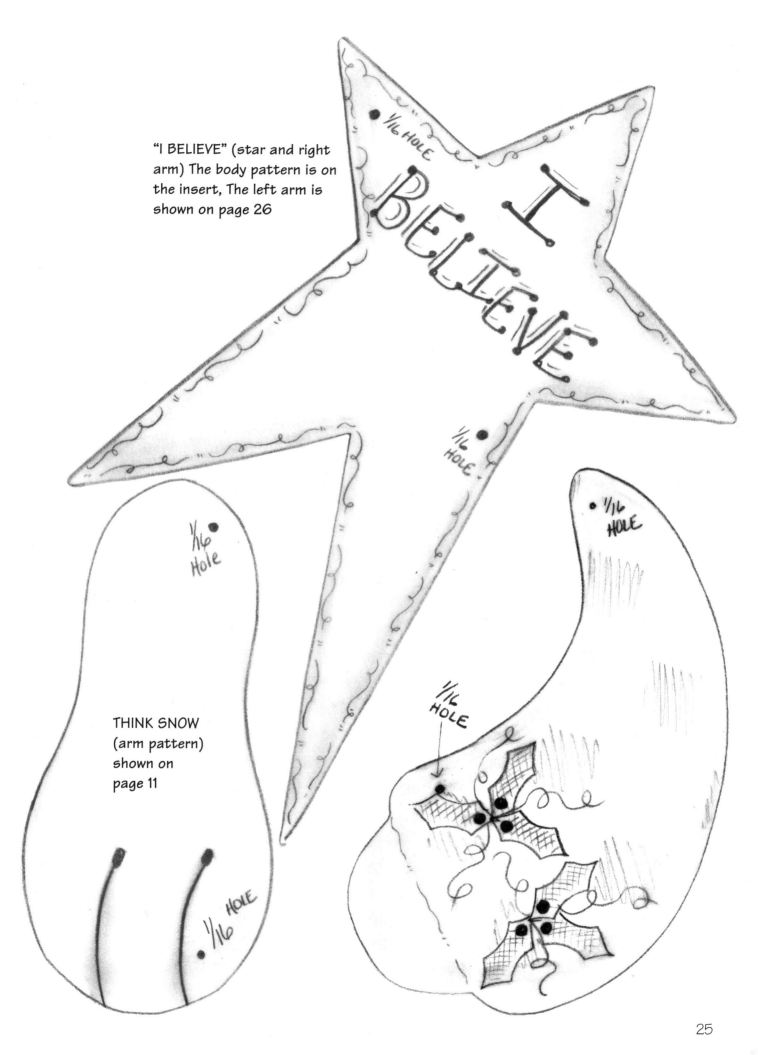

"I BELIEVE" (star and right arm) The body pattern is on the insert, The left arm is shown on page 26

I BELIEVE

¹⁄₁₆ HOLE

¹⁄₁₆ HOLE

¹⁄₁₆ Hole

¹⁄₁₆ HOLE

THINK SNOW
(arm pattern)
shown on
page 11

¹⁄₁₆ HOLE

¹⁄₁₆ HOLE

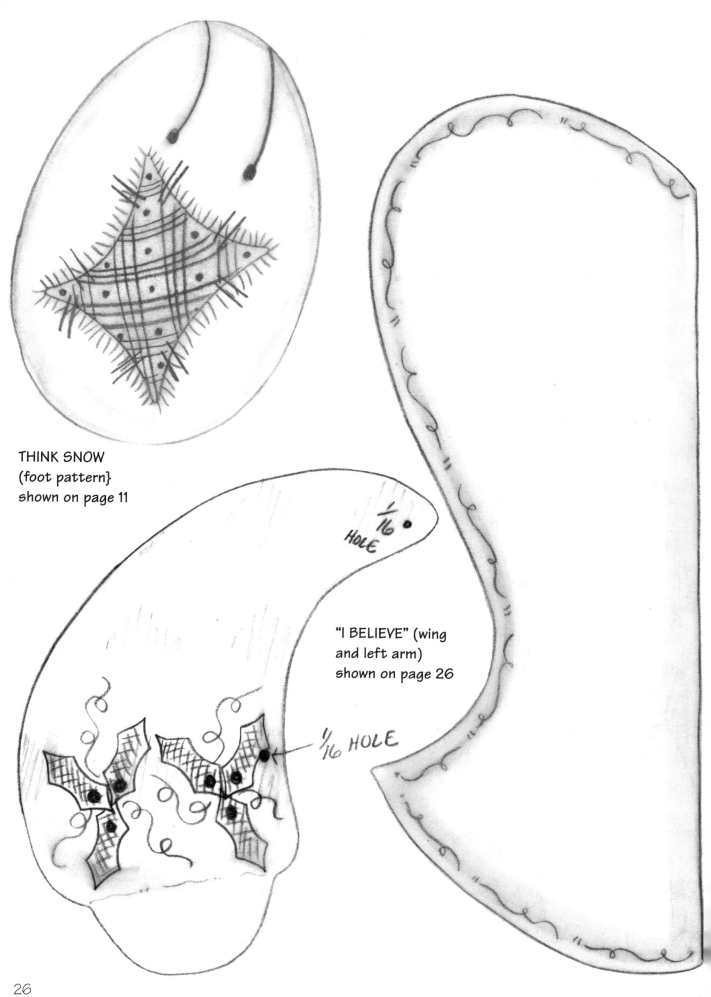

THINK SNOW
(foot pattern}
shown on page 11

"I BELIEVE" (wing
and left arm)
shown on page 26

1/16
HOLE

1/16 HOLE